Easy Instrumental Duets — CLARINETS

Disney SONGS FOR TWO

Disney Characters and Artwork TM & © 2018 Disney

*TARZAN® Owned by Edgar Rice Burroughs, Inc. And Used by Permission © Burroughs/Disney

The following songs are the property of:

Bourne Co.
Music Publishers
5 West 37th Street
New York, NY 10018

HEIGH-HO
SOME DAY MY PRINCE WILL COME
WHEN YOU WISH UPON A STAR
WHISTLE WHILE YOU WORK
WHO'S AFRAID OF THE BIG BAD WOLF?

Arrangements by Mark Phillips

ISBN 978-1-5400-3709-1

HAL•LEONARD®

For all works contained herein:
Unauthorized copying, arranging, adapting, recording, Internet posting, public performance, or other distribution of the music in this publication is an infringement of copyright. Infringers are liable under the law.

Visit Hal Leonard Online at www.halleonard.com

Contact Us:
Hal Leonard
7777 West Bluemound Road
Milwaukee, WI 53213
Email: info@halleonard.com

In Europe contact:
Hal Leonard Europe Limited
42 Wigmore Street
Marylebone, London, W1U 2RN
Email: info@halleonardeurope.com

In Australia contact:
Hal Leonard Australia Pty. Ltd.
4 Lentara Court
Cheltenham, Victoria, 3192 Australia
Email: info@halleonard.com.au

BEAUTY AND THE BEAST
from BEAUTY AND THE BEAST

CLARINETS

Music by ALAN MENKEN
Lyrics by HOWARD ASHMAN

© 1991 Wonderland Music Company, Inc. and Walt Disney Music Company
All Rights Reserved. Used by Permission.

BIBBIDI-BOBBIDI-BOO
(The Magic Song)
from CINDERELLA

CLARINETS

Words by JERRY LIVINGSTON
Music by MACK DAVID
and AL HOFFMAN

Brightly, in 2

© 1948 Walt Disney Music Company
Copyright Renewed.
All Rights Reserved. Used by Permission.

CAN YOU FEEL THE LOVE TONIGHT

from THE LION KING

CLARINETS

Music by ELTON JOHN
Lyrics by TIM RICE

© 1994 Wonderland Music Company, Inc.
All Rights Reserved. Used by Permission.

CHIM CHIM CHER-EE

from MARY POPPINS

CLARINETS

Words and Music by RICHARD M. SHERMAN
and ROBERT B. SHERMAN

© 1964 Wonderland Music Company, Inc.
Copyright Renewed.
All Rights Reserved. Used by Permission.

CIRCLE OF LIFE
from THE LION KING

CLARINETS

Music by ELTON JOHN
Lyrics by TIM RICE

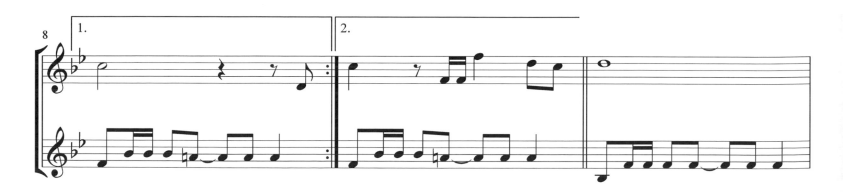

© 1994 Wonderland Music Company, Inc.
All Rights Reserved. Used by Permission.

COLORS OF THE WIND
from POCAHONTAS

CLARINETS

Music by ALAN MENKEN
Lyrics by STEPHEN SCHWARTZ

© 1995 Wonderland Music Company, Inc. and Walt Disney Music Company
All Rights Reserved. Used by Permission.

EVERMORE
from BEAUTY AND THE BEAST

CLARINETS

Music by ALAN MENKEN
Lyrics by TIM RICE

© 2017 Wonderland Music Company, Inc.
All Rights Reserved. Used by Permission.

FRIEND LIKE ME

from ALADDIN

CLARINETS

Music by ALAN MENKEN
Lyrics by HOWARD ASHMAN

© 1992 Wonderland Music Company, Inc. and Walt Disney Music Company
All Rights Reserved. Used by Permission.

HEIGH-HO

The Dwarfs' Marching Song from SNOW WHITE AND THE SEVEN DWARFS

CLARINETS

Words by LARRY MOREY
Music by FRANK CHURCHILL

Copyright © 1938 by Bourne Co. (ASCAP)
Copyright Renewed
International Copyright Secured   All Rights Reserved

HOW FAR I'LL GO

from MOANA

CLARINETS

Music and Lyrics by
LIN-MANUEL MIRANDA

© 2016 Walt Disney Music Company
All Rights Reserved. Used by Permission.

LET IT GO
from FROZEN

CLARINETS

Music and Lyrics by KRISTEN ANDERSON-LOPEZ
and ROBERT LOPEZ

© 2013 Wonderland Music Company, Inc.
All Rights Reserved. Used by Permission.

MICKEY MOUSE MARCH

from THE MICKEY MOUSE CLUB

CLARINETS

Words and Music by
JIMMIE DODD

March tempo

© 1955 Walt Disney Music Company
Copyright Renewed.
All Rights Reserved. Used by Permission.

SOME DAY MY PRINCE WILL COME

from SNOW WHITE AND THE SEVEN DWARFS

CLARINETS

Words by LARRY MOREY
Music by FRANK CHURCHILL

Copyright © 1937 by Bourne Co. (ASCAP)
Copyright Renewed
International Copyright Secured   All Rights Reserved

SOMETHING THERE

from BEAUTY AND THE BEAST

CLARINETS

Music by ALAN MENKEN
Lyrics by HOWARD ASHMAN

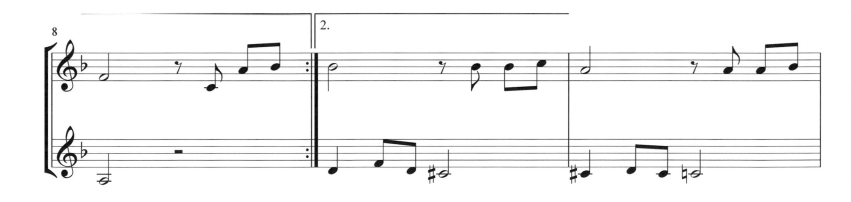

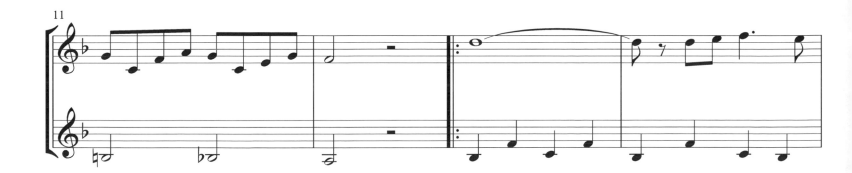

© 1991 Wonderland Music Company, Inc. and Walt Disney Music Company
All Rights Reserved. Used by Permission.

SUPERCALIFRAGILISTICEXPIALIDOCIOUS

from MARY POPPINS

CLARINETS

Words and Music by RICHARD M. SHERMAN
and ROBERT B. SHERMAN

© 1964 Wonderland Music Company, Inc.
Copyright Renewed.
All Rights Reserved. Used by Permission.

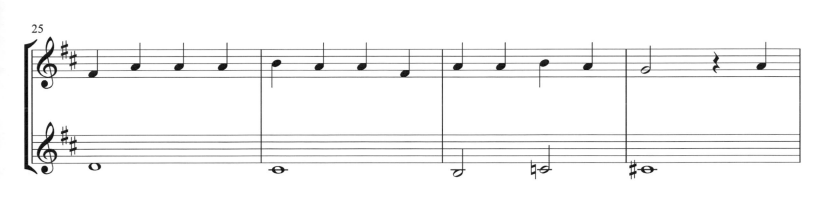

D.C. al Fine

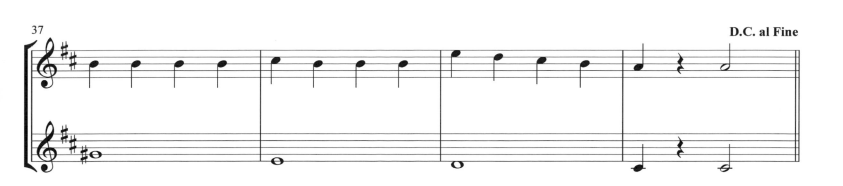

WHEN SHE LOVED ME

from TOY STORY 2

CLARINETS

Music and Lyrics by
RANDY NEWMAN

© 1999 Walt Disney Music Company and Pixar Talking Pictures
All Rights Reserved. Used by Permission.

WHEN YOU WISH UPON A STAR

from PINOCCHIO

CLARINETS

Words by NED WASHINGTON
Music by LEIGH HARLINE

Moderately

Copyright © 1940 by Bourne Co. (ASCAP)
Copyright Renewed
International Copyright Secured   All Rights Reserved

WHISTLE WHILE YOU WORK

from SNOW WHITE AND THE SEVEN DWARFS

CLARINETS

Words by LARRY MOREY
Music by FRANK CHURCHILL

Moderately, in 2

Copyright © 1937 by Bourne Co. (ASCAP)
Copyright Renewed
International Copyright Secured   All Rights Reserved

WHO'S AFRAID OF THE BIG BAD WOLF?

from THREE LITTLE PIGS

CLARINETS

Words and Music by
FRANK CHURCHILL
Additional Lyric by ANN RONELL

Copyright © 1933 by Bourne Co. (ASCAP)
Copyright Renewed
International Copyright Secured   All Rights Reserved

A WHOLE NEW WORLD

from ALADDIN

CLARINETS

Music by ALAN MENKEN
Lyrics by TIM RICE

© 1992 Wonderland Music Company, Inc. and Walt Disney Music Company
All Rights Reserved. Used by Permission.

YOU'LL BE IN MY HEART

(Pop Version)
from TARZAN®

Words and Music by
PHIL COLLINS

CLARINETS

Moderately

© 1999 Edgar Rice Burroughs, Inc. and Walt Disney Music Company
All Rights Reserved. Used by Permission.
TARZAN® Owned by Edgar Rice Burroughs, Inc. and Used by Permission.
© Burroughs/Disney

YOU'RE WELCOME

from MOANA

CLARINETS

Music and Lyrics by
LIN-MANUEL MIRANDA

© 2016 Walt Disney Music Company
All Rights Reserved. Used by Permission.

ZIP-A-DEE-DOO-DAH

from SONG OF THE SOUTH

CLARINETS

Words by RAY GILBERT
Music by ALLIE WRUBEL

© 1945 Walt Disney Music Company
Copyright Renewed.
All Rights Reserved. Used by Permission.